Joe Biden

Introduction

Are you a Joe Biden's die hard supporter and are curious to know more about him, from his early days, even before he joined politics, to the time he first entered politics, his long, highly decorated long term career, his time as the vice president under Barack Obama and more?

And are you looking for a guide that is not only easy to follow but fun filled and based on verifiable facts?

If you've answered YES, keep reading...

This book will give you an in-depth understanding of Joe Biden, the 46th President of the United States!

Joe Biden has been a darling for many voters across the United States. His long career in politics, which spans from 1970s speaks for itself. And without a doubt, Americans are about to benefit from his wealth of experience serving in different high level positions in government, his professional background and his passion to see all Americans, from the poor to the middle class and working Americans to live better lives.

By virtue that you are reading this, it is clear you are already sold to Biden and perhaps are looking to know more about him more than the fact that he was Obama's Vice President. You probably want to be able to hold intelligent conversations when talking about him.

Perhaps you are wondering...

How was Joe Biden in his childhood years?

Was he always interested in politics?

What about his education and professional life – what did he study and when?

When did he join politics and what was it like in the initial years in politics?

Does he have any scandals and other dirty linen?

How has his life in politics been?

Does he have a family – how is his family life like?

What are his biggest wins and biggest loses to-date?

If you have these and other related questions, this book is for you so keep reading, as it covers the ins and outs of Joe Biden's life inside out.

Let's begin!

Table of Contents

WORLD CHANGING HISTORY

MANSA MUSA AND TIMBUKTU

A FASCINATING HISTORY
FROM BEGINNING TO END

Chapter 1: Early Life

History records that 20 November 1942 was the hottest day of the month, with daytime temperatures reaching a staggering 67.3 degrees F and averaging at 32.7 degrees during the night. We celebrate this date primarily as the day when the Siege of Malta ended. A strategically located island at the height of World War 2, Malta served as a base for British sea and air forces from which the Allies could easily disrupt Axis ships transporting reinforcements and essential supplies from Europe to North Africa. Had the Axis managed to gain control of the island, Nazi Germany and Fascist Italy would have likely maintained their hold on North Africa. The war would have probably ended very differently.

No doubt, all that is important, but there is another reason 20 November 1942 is a special day. On this hot, busy Friday, a newlywed couple Joseph Robinette Biden and Catherine Eugenia Biden, gave birth to a bouncing baby boy at St. Mary's Hospital in Scranton, Pennsylvania. They named the boy who was their first child after his father: Joseph Robinette Biden (Jr.). Joseph R. Biden Jr. would go on to become the 47th Vice President of the United States of America under President Barack Obama, and the Democratic party's frontrunner for the U.S. presidency in 2020.

Life as a young boy for Joe Biden was full of ups and downs. Although his parents had slightly different heritages (Joseph Biden Sr. had Irish, English, and French roots while Catherine Eugenia was Irish), theirs was a predominantly Catholic family. Growing up as an Irish Catholic kid in the 40s to 60s was tricky. It was the period of the Vietnam war, the civil rights movement, and Vatican II or the Second Vatican Council announced on 25 January 1959 by Pope John XIII in a bid to regain Christian unity.

During this time, Joe Biden attended parochial schools that had nuns as the teachers. It is here that Joe credits as the inspiration for his regard for basic human dignity, a vital social principle in the Catholic Church. These Catholic roots also helped him understand the importance of solidarity, especially among the working class and the poor, which he often cites when discussing economic policies and job security. When the U.S electorate elected him alongside Barack Obama, he became the first Catholic vice president in U.S. history.

The rise and fall of his father, Joe Biden Sr., may have also had a hand in how Joe Biden designs his economic policies. When he was young, Biden Sr. was considerably wealthy. His father, Joseph H. Biden (Joe's grandfather), was an oil businessman while working for a company that manufactured sealants for marine ships during WWII. He had money, drove fast cars, sailed yachts, and flew airplanes.

Everything changed drastically after the war. Work was hard to come by just as he had gotten married and had Joe Biden Jr., and things would even get worse in the years that followed. The family fell into hardship. When Joe Biden was 10, Joe Sr. walked into his room with a gloomy face and told him they had to give up their home in Scranton, Pennsylvania, and relocate to Delaware in search of work. The family ended up in Claymont, Delaware, where Joe Biden Sr. initially worked as a car salesman. Joe spent most of his holidays and summers in the next 12 years with his grandparents (on his mother's side) back at Scranton.

This phase was particularly significant for Joe Biden Sr. In just one decade, he had found himself living in a 2-bedroom apartment in a drab, soulless suburb in Delaware, selling second-hand cars to support his wife and four kids. Joe saw hints of his father's former self in his wardrobe, in the form of posh clothes and a perfect pocket square. He also kept a polo mallet and polished boots at the back of his closest, right behind his riding pinks.

Despite his fall from grace, Joe Biden Sr. had a resilient spirit. He believed that man's true measure is not how often he gets knocked down, but how quickly he can get up. This lesson resonated profoundly with Joe Biden Jr. Amid these difficulties; he learned an important lesson from his father. A job could signify more than just a paycheck; it could embody both respect and dignity.

In his autobiography, Joe expounds this by recounting a story about his father resigning from one of his jobs because it went against his morals, even though he needed the money. This happened when the owner, who often rewarded his customers and employees with silver dollars, decided to spill a bucket of silvers on the dance floor during a Christmas party at the dealership. His employees scrambled to collect them at his amusement.

As a child, Joe Jr. was a popular kid, but he had a stuttering problem that he struggled to overcome. He became incredibly aggressive when people teased him about it.

After a few years in Claymont, the Bidens moved to Wilmington and stayed there until the kids were grown up. The family was doing okay now, so Joe and his two brothers were able to enroll in the prestigious Archmere Academy. Valerie Biden Owens, the younger sister, attended Ursuline Academy, a girls-only Catholic school.

It is during his time at Archmere that Joe Biden Jr. managed to beat his stutter. He would stand in front of a mirror and recite memorized passages repeatedly until he could do it without stuttering. This stutter sometimes appears when he is giving a speech in public.

At Archmere, Joe Jr. was an average student but an outstanding athlete, especially after a sudden growth spurt in his mid-teenage years. Despite having a skinny physique, he was a spectacular pass receiver, and his football coach (E. John Walsh) regarded him as one of the best receivers he had seen in his 16 years of coaching.

Biden later enlisted in the University of Delaware, where he focused on girls, football, and late-night gab sessions. In his junior year, he flew to the Bahamas for his spring break and met a student from Syracuse University called Neilia Hunter. Neilia came from a well-off family in New York, and at the moment, she was just relaxing on a beach in the Bahamas. According to Joe, it was love at first glance. Right there and then, he set out to pursue her with the same vigor he has always shown in his political career. He decided to enroll in Syracuse Law School after graduation just to get closer to her.

During his first year at Syracuse, Biden failed a class for not citing properly the source to a law article. He was able to retake the course after claiming that the borrowing was not intentional, but he still finished almost at the bottom of the class. This mistake proved costly when plagiarism charges were brought against him in 1987, subsequently sabotaging his presidential campaign.

After law school, Biden went back to Wilmington with Neilia as his bride and then married her in 1966. As he did not want to join corporate practice and criminal defense was not paying enough, Joe resorted to politics.

Chapter 2 - Law School, Senate Race and Tragic

In 1970, Joe Biden Jr. achieved his first significant political milestone when he got into the New Castle County Council. After two years, at just 29 years of age, local politicians from the Democratic party nominated Biden to run against the extremely popular 2-term Senator J. Caleb Boggs in the U.S. Senate, as a sacrificial lamb. According to the constitution, you have to be at least 30 years old to claim the seat. Joe's 30th birthday fell just before the scheduling of the new Congress to start in January.

At the time, Joe Biden was only an inexperienced lawyer who had just won his first seat on the New Castle County Council. He was young and eager to try his luck against Republican Senator Caleb Boggs in the upcoming 1972 elections. On the other hand, Caleb Boggs was one of Delaware's most popular politicians in the history of the state. It was a classic David vs. Goliath contest.

Biden turned to county aide Vince D'Anna for advice as well as the county councilman who had encouraged him to run for public office in the first place and anyone else who could be able to assess his chances. They were all equally befuddled, and the response was unanimous: he must be out of his mind! He was unknown and untested, betting on a perceived desire for change to overwhelm the comfort of voting for a familiar face.

In November 1971, at a downstate event some days before the official announcement, Joe revealed that he was running for Senate, only to change his statement later during the day to say that he was only 90 percent sure. He subsequently stated that he just wanted to confirm support from a few places before making his decision. This apparent sense of reluctance earned him a spot in the papers, with The Morning News joking about his slip-up with the headline: "Biden to [oops] MAY try Senate." Let us just say; he was off to a rough start.

At the start of the New Year, Biden joked that his winning chances were about 5-to-1 in Boggs' favour. Indeed, even the thought that he could unseat an undefeated politician such as Caleb Boggs was unfathomable at the time. The popular opinion was that the incumbent Senator would continue his winning streak for the third term.

Boggs was regarded as the lovable old man in Delaware politics, thanks mostly to the image of the sweet grandpa he had managed to create for himself. He was pro-business and had previously gotten support from labour. None of the "realistic" prospects from the Democrats was interested in running against him, which is why it was easy for Biden to get the nomination. The Democratic Party was more focused on getting the governor's seat. Further, the position of Joe in the county council had been absorbed into a Republican district, so he did not have a future there. That aside, Joe was confident because he did not have much to lose.

There was also a moment when it seemed like Boggs would not actually run for re-election. According to William Hildebrand, Boggs' former aide, the senator had decided not to stand again as far back as 1968. However, the Republican powers from above, including President Nixon himself, intervened and told him to run to boost turnout for the gubernatorial race. The president was particularly concerned about a possibly divisive primary between Republican Pete du Pont and Wilmington Mayor Hal Haskell for the party's Senate nomination if Boggs' failed to run. Ever the party man, Boggs reluctantly agreed to stand once more, expecting to glide seamlessly through the elections.

On the other hand, Biden was busy meeting and interacting with voters about ten times a day in a bid to market himself. Another factor that Biden could utilize was that this would be the first election in which 18-year olds could vote. Biden was young and, therefore, much more capable of connecting with younger voters. During the race, he mobilized an army of at least 150 young professionals, college, and high school students who worked day and night for him from June to 4 November.

Biden aimed to spend as little as possible during the 1972 campaign, targeting an expenditure of around $100,000 to $150,000, which meant minimizing T.V. advertising and paid literature distribution. Instead, he would rely primarily on family and friends, and a little help from a Boston-based media consultant to organize young volunteers to hand-deliver the campaign's literature throughout the state. Once a week, during the weekends, the army of volunteers would hand-deliver private campaign newspapers to various Delaware households. By mid-October, the papers had reached up to 85 percent of all households. At some point, people would literally be waiting at their doors for a kid to deliver the advertisements.

When making his speeches, Biden would target the young audience to get them to vote for him and convince their parents to change their minds. In a later statement, Valerie Biden, who was influential in recruiting the army of young volunteers, said that this strategy determined the election's outcome. She attributed it to feedback from parents who stated that anyone who could get their child to wake up at 6 a.m. on a Saturday to hand-deliver campaign materials ahead of their 10 o'clock football game in school deserved a second look because there must be something special about him.

Joe avoided crossing the liberal line while harnessing the youth energy by steering away from the student activists of that time. In fact, he was so afraid of being associated with the then liberal Democratic Presidential aspirant George McGovern that he actively set out to distance himself from the left. He emphasized that the root of his campaign was his army of volunteers and not McGovern's institution. He thus shied away from culture war debates. Instead, he always tried to redirect conversations to the pocketbook or local issues such as protecting Social Security, corporate loopholes in income tax, the environment, and crime.

On several issues, he would always look for a stance that would please liberals without alienating the undecided voters. For example, in one of his campaigns, he said that the authorities should treat marijuana possession as a minor offense or misdemeanour, although he did not support its legalization. Joe also claimed that the police should concentrate their efforts more on combating heroin instead. Also, he did not support the Vietnam War and repeatedly criticized Boggs for failing to stand up to Richard Nixon to end it. He believed it was an awful waste of money, time, and lives on a flawed premise.

Biden also trod carefully when it came to race-related matters. He had called for more public housing as a councilman, but he also insisted he did not wholly agree with the far left on racial issues. This tendency to avoid taking a firm position on specific issues earned Biden some eye-rolls, with some analysts calling him more of a conservative than a democrat.

The good news is that he did not need to use abstract political insight to influence the youth. The girls freely admitted that he was appealing while the young men admired his "new hero" appearance when he talked about how old Boggs had messed things up. If anything, Biden's tendency to assume middle-ground positions actually helped win over young people who were also middle-of-the-road voters.

Boggs underestimated the intensity of the challenge until it was too late. Where Biden lacked in experience, he compensated for with a good image. He presented the image of a young family man with an attractive wife and three beautiful children. He was also smart, funny, charming, a good speaker, and free of scandals. All of these qualities and factors combined ultimately saw Joe Biden pull off the political upset of a lifetime when he won the Delaware Senate seat at only 29 years by just over 3,000 votes.

The country was abuzz with this extraordinary accomplishment. Even the sports columns hailed this victory, with headlines congratulating the "old quarterback" on his way to the Senate. Indeed, for a boy who had grown up with so many challenges, it seemed like things were finally going right. He was a young man with a beautiful family and a promising political career.

Unfortunately, as fate would have it, Joe Biden's celebrations for the 1972 win would be short-lived by a tragic event. A few days before Christmas, while on a shopping trip with the family car – a Chevrolet station wagon – a tractor-trailer broadsided Joe Biden's wife Neilia and the kids in a tragic accident. Neilia and the couple's youngest and only daughter, Naomi, died almost instantly. Naomi was just 13 months old while Neilia was 30 when she passed away. Their two sons, Beau and Hunter Biden, who were three and four years old respectively, sustained serious injuries. Joe had to hold his swearing-in ceremony at their bedside as a result. Suddenly the young senator-elect was a single father with two little kids.

Chapter 3 - Time in Senate, Remarriage, What did he vote as Senator

Joe was in a dark place following his wife and daughter's deaths. During his later interviews, he credited his second wife, Jill, as the rock that helped him through that difficult time. However, the love story of Biden and Jill did not start as sweet. When the couple met for the first time in 1975, they were at completely different points in their lives. On the one hand, Joe was a widower who had lost his wife and young daughter just three years prior, to a tragic accident that had left their two sons, Beau and Hunter, in critical condition. On the other hand, Jill was just about to graduate from the University of Delaware and was thinking about her future. Frank, Biden's brother, was the one who made the introductions.

In an interview in 2016, Jill admitted that when he first saw Joe on their blind date, she did not think it would work. She was a senior who had been dating guys in T-shirts, clogs, and jeans, and here was Joe, all dressed up in loafers and a sport coat, and to top it all off, he was 9 years older!

But when they went to a Philadelphian movie theatre to watch A Man and a Woman, they developed a connection. When he took her back home that night, Joe shook her hand, and Jill went upstairs to call her mom at 1:00 at night to tell her she had finally met a gentleman.

At the time, Biden was raising his two sons on his own, but Jill quickly became a member of the family. Soon she and the kids had grown attached to each other, and before long, Joe was contemplating the idea of remarriage. According to him, it was Hunter and Beau who first brought up the subject. Biden was shaving one morning when Hunter approached him and told him that Beau thought the two should get married. Biden responded that it was a pretty good idea.

Unfortunately, Jill was not thinking about marriage at the time. In fact, Joe proposed up to 5 times before she said yes. She later revealed that her reluctance to accept the proposal was not because she did not love Joe. It was her concern about the kids that made her think that it was not the right time.

She felt that it was too soon after their mother's death, so she had to wait until she was sure she would be committed to the marriage.

The couple ultimately held their wedding in New York on 17 June 1977 at the United Nations chapel. The ceremony was low key, with about 40 close friends and family in attendance, including Hunter and Beau, who joined the couple at their honeymoon to further enhance their family bond. When Jill and Joe had their first child, a bouncing baby girl, Beau and Hunter chose their little sister's name: Ashley.

During his first years as a senator, Joe Biden was a key activist of environmental issues and consumer protection and called for more government accountability. In a Time magazine profile at around 1974, he was named in the 200 Faces for the Future, describing him as "compulsively ambitious" and "self-confident" after his tragic family loss. His foreign policy made him one of the most respected foreign policy experts, ultimately becoming the Committee on Foreign Relations chairman for several years.

Biden's short run in the County Council had established him as a sharp liberal politician. He was genuinely worried about environmental degradation and poverty and was willing to stand against corporate interests. He opposed the creation of oil refineries and fought to protect crucial wetlands. He also spoke against destroying tidal marshes and attempted to prevent a controversial superhighway he dubbed a "ten-lane monstrosity" from being constructed.

In addition, Biden called out a public housing report for failing to address the poorest of the poorest and was outraged when there was bulldozing of poor black residents' homes. With an eye on the balance between the preservation and growth of the country's natural resources, Joe was keen to curb development or, if possible, de-escalate it. As such, he promoted mass transit instead of the construction of the "senseless highways."

Although he was a relatively standard liberal politician, Joe Biden stood out for his general lack of filter. He was a gifted speaker and used this to his advantage, speaking out controversial and sometimes inflammatory lines that build up his reputation as an unrepentant truth-teller. He quickly adopted the controversial practice of making paid speeches, usually at high schools, colleges, and fundraisers, to supplement his salary. As a result, he earned tens of thousands of dollars on top of his yearly income as a senator, marking his debut as a prolific and highly paid speaker.

Biden also sided with Israel from the start. During the senate campaign, he was hit by a mini-scandal when it was discovered that he had instructed a graduate student under him not to include the candidate's personal views in a policy paper for the Middle East because it would be tantamount to committing "political suicide." Biden virtually denied the claims, stating that he was just playing the devil's advocate amidst the debate over a settlement in which Israel would have to return its illegally-occupied land after the '67 war. He would spend his career showing overwhelming support to Israel and was instrumental in providing the country with significant U.S. aid.

Meanwhile, the Watergate scandal, which had rocked Washington since 1972, revealed Joe's strong belief in unity, consensus, and bipartisanship. He warned against celebrating the GOP drop under the Republican Party, saying that the party's failure would also affect the Democrats. He disliked wholly blaming the Republicans for Watergate, emphasizing the role of political institutions in keeping the people together and putting the blame on the GOP to compromise the system. After delaying his stance on impeachment, Biden finally delivered a thoroughly prepared speech in April 1974. In it, he called for people to be fair to Nixon, attacking government leakers and the press, as well as their sources. He argued that impeachment was an important matter not to be left to the press.

In 1974, a court panel found that state education and housing policies were designed to segregate the predominantly white suburbs and the predominantly black school systems in Wilmington, Delaware. White residents in the suburbs were concerned about the idea of following a busing plan even before the court had enforced a busing program.

Biden, who had campaigned for busing while running against the incumbent Senator Caleb Boggs in 1972, was in a dilemma. After some protest from his constituents, Biden had to rethink his stance. In 1973 and 1974, he began to side with anti-busing measures. In 1974, he voted against an anti-busing policy known as the Gurney Amendment, which would have blocked the federal court from using busing plans and disrupted other court-mandated desegregation efforts. Biden's vote put a stop on the measure before it could even reach the Senate.

Biden stated that he opposed the measure because it would have opened the door for anyone with a civil rights case from back to 1954 to revisit their case. In a television interview in 1975, he added that 90% of those court cases were not connected to busing and that that would have led to chaos in the court system. He supported an amendment proposed by Senator Jesse Helms (of North Carolina), who was firmly against desegregation efforts and civil rights legislation. This amendment would put an end to the practice of collecting racial statistics about teachers and students by the Department of Health, Education, & Welfare, as well as the classification of teachers and students by race.

Biden argued that the concept of busing was bankrupt and that the Senate should shift its focus to providing minority groups in America with better educational opportunities. The Helms amendment was not successful, but Joe subsequently introduced a similar proposal barring school systems from using the 36 billion-dollar education bill to assign students and teachers to schools based on their race. This basically meant that no child, whether white or black, would be segregated by "some faceless bureaucrat."

The amendment passed, stirring outrage from Edward Brooke, the Massachusetts Republican who was the only senator of colour at the time. Brooke argued that the proposal went against civil rights. The measure laid the foundation for Joe Biden's policy on anti-busing legislation. He approached the issue with a conservative view, using terms such as "forced busing" while his colleagues emphasized desegregation instead of transportation.

Over the last four decades, Joe has always maintained that he was right on his position on busing. He said that he was mainly against busing in terms of de facto segregation, which simply means unofficial segregation treated like it happened 'naturally.' He added that busing was okay only when it came to de jure, which is when the law directly and intentionally enforces segregation.

Let us now look at Biden's 1988-failed run:

Chapter 4 - Failed 1988 Run

When Joe won the race to the Senate against Boggs in 1972, many people considered him Presidential material. There was a lot of excitement surrounding his campaign, with TIME noting that he would just about be eligible to run for the White House in 1976, by around two months. Joe contemplated the idea but did not declare his interest until 9 June 1987, about one decade later. The good news was that he was still young and in his prime, which was a key strength.

During the 1980s, Biden was considered different from his fellow Democrats; they say him as a bright new hope for the country's leadership. At the time, he was just 44 years old, giving motivational speeches while exuding youthful energy. He hoped to show off his skill as chairman of the Judiciary Committee during the confirmation hearings for the Supreme Court nomination of conservative Robert Bork (the hearings of which Biden was in charge). The hearings would boost his presidential campaign by giving him a platform to market himself on national T.V.

However, things did not turn out as Biden had expected. Just a few days to the Bork hearings, a video was released showing how Biden had plagiarized a speech by Neil Kinnock (U.K. Labour Party leader) without attributing him. Little more digging revealed prior examples of plagiarism from the senator, and the scandal became more popular than his role in the confirmation hearings.

People now began to perceive him as a candidate of style, rather than substance. The Kinnock scandal was particularly bad because it reinforced prior concerns that Biden was just a vessel for others' ideas. Some critics even claimed that he did not attribute Kinnock because he was on autopilot and did not even understand the speech's context. Reporters piled on with more research showing that Biden had also plagiarized Humphrey and Robert Kennedy without providing the proper citation. The incident in 1965 at Syracuse Law School came to light too, where Biden had failed a course for using five pages from a law review article without accrediting the source.

These offenses, by themselves, would have been irrelevant without the Kinnock saga.

When there was a press conference for Biden to explain himself, he failed to convince the public by contradicting himself, saying that it was illogical to accredit every political idea. The final nail in the coffin came when footage showing Biden bragging about his academic accomplishments, claiming that he had graduated from law school in the top half of his class when he was actually 76th out of 85 was discovered.

On 24 September 1987, Biden announced he was stepping out of the presidential race. Biden later gave Kinnock a few of his speeches in an attempt to make things even. About two decades later, he admitted in his memoir – Promises to Keep -- that he was to blame for the plagiarism scandal. He revealed that although he had credited Kinnock repeatedly off the record, he should have done it officially at the State Fair debate.

The attack video turned out to have originated from Massachusetts Governor Michael Dukakis, who was one of his main opponents in the presidential bid. Dukakis initially denied the allegation but ultimately confessed to the leakage. This revelation was particularly surprising because people knew the governor as a "straight arrow" who preferred to use positive campaigning tactics. In the end, Paul Tully and John Sasso, two of Dukakis' aides, decided to step down for lying to TIME.

This roller coaster of events outraged the public, with both of the candidates being deemed dishonest. Biden, in particular, was accused of lying even when he did not need to. Dukakis found himself in trouble again when he rehired John Sasso a year later. This was just after a goofy photo showing Dukakis in a military tank was leaked, painting him as someone who was not serious about national security issues. George H.W. Bush, who was running with the Republican Party, ultimately won the election.

Biden's brief 1988 presidential campaign would have a long-term impact on political journalism and political campaigns in the future. In a 1987 essay on TIME, Walter Shapiro argued that the campaign had seen political reporters turn into "character cops" who traded in pop psychology and paparazzi politics.

However, stepping out of the presidential race turned out to be a good thing for Joe Biden, after all. In February 1988, doctors discovered that he had a brain aneurysm after experiencing a stubborn headache. He had surgery to remove the aneurysm and had to undergo operation again to remove another secondary aneurysm that had formed. The doctors said that the condition would have probably killed him had he stayed in the race.

Back in 1987, before announcing his candidacy, Biden had consulted his son Hunter (who was now a teenager) on whether he should run for the presidency. Hunter was optimistic, telling him that he could not see him doing it any other time. Of course, Hunter was wrong. Biden rain again in 2008 for the Democratic Party nomination, but lost to Barack Obama.

Chapter 5 - Time in Senate from 1988 to 2008

In 1987, just a few months before his first presidential campaign, Joe Biden became the Senate Judiciary Committee chairman. His main objective in this role was to enforce legislation that would gradually lead to a reduced crime rate.

Before he became chairman, Joe had been influential in passing two bills that established mandatory minimum punishments for drug offenses. Now, under severe scrutiny from the Republicans accusing his party of being lenient on crime at the peak of the crack cocaine epidemic and high violent crime rates, Biden was looking for holistic reform. These conditions ultimately led to the enactment of the Violent Crime Control & Law Enforcement Act in 1994 by the then-President Bill Clinton.

In the decades leading up to the enactment, the rate of violent crimes had been rising progressively, finally peaking in 1991. By the time of the bill's passing, violent crime rate had increased by 39% from 1983-1993. The bill received overwhelming support from the Democratic Party, with the Senate passing the bill by a staggering 95 to 4 vote. In the last conference report, only 2 Democrats voted no. The House passed the final bill with a 235 to 195 vote, with the supporting Democrats surpassing those opposing it by almost three times.

In addition, although with a little influence from President Bill Clinton, the Congressional Black Caucus was mostly in support of the legislation. Almost 40 religious leaders from the African American community also came out to support the bill with the hope of "saving their communities and their children."

The bill, apart from establishing mandatory sentencing for repeat offenders, set out to:

- Ban federal assault weapons

- Disband gang memberships

- Offer grants for expanding and constructing correctional facilities to states that enforced the mandatory sentencing

- Create sixty new offenses punishable by death under 41 capital statutes, for example, civil rights murders, the murder of federal law enforcement officers, and acts of terrorism.

Today, however, many consider the law as a significant contributor to mass incarceration. As a result, policymakers who helped push the legislation have received a lot of criticism, including Joe Biden. One of the most significant impacts of the legislation was that it enticed states to expand or build more correctional facilities. The bill's federal money prompted cities and states to make more arrests and increase incarceration and prosecutions, and some people are still serving sentences enforced by the bill.

However, one of the many issues that Joseph R. Biden got right was his foreign policy on Bosnia. In spring 1992, Bosnia came under attack from Serbia and its proxies. At the time, the new country had just come out of an unfavourable period. The arms embargo imposed by the U.N froze Serbia's military superiority, while Bosnia lost the ability to defend itself.

European mediators decided to intervene. Back in America, several members of Congress and senators mobilized to discuss the Bosnian situation. They were concerned that Bush and the then Clinton administration were too nonchalant about their stand on Bosnia. They saw it fit to lift the arms embargo and provide military support to Bosnia.

Senator Bob Dole took charge of the campaign, leading with a forceful and consistent approach. Senator Joseph Lieberman provided the back up with a bipartisan spirit. Joe Biden was on the campaign too, and, like the others, he was eager to resolve the situation. In September 1992, he sponsored an amendment that exempted Bosnia from the U.N. embargo because it served to empower the aggressor. In the amendment, the U.S. president would be able to provide Bosnia with the much-needed military assistance after lifting of the embargo.

When debating about Bosnia in the Senate, Biden was supportive. He provided a clear image of the situation on the ground with precise and informed questions and comments. In June 1993, in an op-ed in the New York Times, Biden called out the appeasement on Bosnia by the U.N. and added that there was a need to beef up security in the country's safe areas. To show their determination, Biden and his compatriot Dole flew to Sarajevo, the capital of the besieged Bosnia-Herzegovina, on early June 1994.

At the beginning of the following year, Biden, Dole, and Lieberman co-sponsored a bill aimed at lifting the arms embargo. This led to the passing of the Bosnia & Herzegovina Self Defence Act in 1995, which was highly influential in resolving the Bosnian war.

Chapter 6: Second Run and Obama's Vp

After several decades in the Senate, Joe Biden decided to try his luck at the White House for the second time in 2007. This time, he had more experience and stood a chance to become the first Roman Catholic president after John F. Kennedy – if elected. What's more, he would be the only president in history who was a child of World War II.

His campaign revolved around his plan to resolve the Iraq War using a system of federalization. Before he declared his candidacy, Biden had been talking about running for president for months. Some sources suggested that he would accept the Secretary of State's job and drop out because he had vast experience and credentials in foreign affairs. However, he outrightly refused this and said that his eyes were on the presidency. He officially joined the race on 31 January 2007 with a quick attack on frontrunner Hillary Clinton, challenging her plan for the Iraq War. He criticized her for proposing a "military solution" instead of a "political solution." He also criticized the Bush administration for its position on Iraq.

Earlier in 2002, Biden had suggested legislation that would prevent the president from authorizing the war. When the legislation failed in the Senate, he stated that the president should emphasize that the troops would not get in the middle of a civil war. Instead, they would train the Iraqi forces and prevent al Qaeda from claiming chunks of territory.

In April 2007, the Delaware Senator called out John McCain (the Republican presidential candidate) for supporting the surge approach in Iraq, calling it a "failed policy." He argued that although violence had gone down in Iraq, there was still no political change because the Iraqi people did not trust their government. This perceived desire to change the Iraq War approach was the cornerstone of Biden's presidential campaign in 2007.

During his first presidential debate, Biden said that the question was not whether the U.S. had won or lost the war, but whether they could extract the troops without leaving chaos. He went on to describe his system of federalism, which involved decentralizing Iraq and letting them decide their destiny.

Biden shifted his focus from Iraq momentarily when the genocide in Darfur, Sudan peaked, prompting President George W. Bush to enforce economic sanctions against the country until its government ended the genocide. Biden supported the move and insisted on more involvement from the United States forces, even putting a No-Fly Zone over the region.

On 3 June, Joe resumed back to the War in Iraq, discussing his vote to continue funding the troops. He later added that it was unrealistic to expect all troops' redeployment and then criticized the president for going into the war without a winning or exit plan.

On 23 October, Joe unveiled his proposed health care plan, which entailed expanding coverage for everyone without mandating complete universal coverage. The aim was to encourage wellness and modernize treatment at the cost of about $80-110 billion per year. This, he said, he would achieve by eliminating tax cuts for dividends, capital gains, and the wealthiest 1%. The SCHIP program would also include children who were 300% above the poverty line.

Further, following the assassination of Benazir Bhutto, former prime minister of Pakistan, Biden got the opportunity to gain some momentum by displaying his foreign policy experience. He spoke about the situation in Pakistan and his proposal to protect the nation's nuclear weapons. Unfortunately, this would not be enough to secure his nomination with the Democratic Party. On 3 January 2008, after gathering only 1% of the total vote in the Iowa caucus to wind up in a daunting fifth place, Biden stepped out of the presidential race. In the company of his close friends and family at a tearful rally, he comforted his supporters by announcing that he would still resume his role in the senate as the Foreign Relations Committee chairman.

Looking back, several factors led to the collapse of Joe Biden's second presidential bid. One of the biggest challenges was that Biden's popularity had dwindled significantly since his first historical win against Boggs in 1972. In 2007, he was relatively unknown. According to a Gallup poll conducted between April 2-5, 38% of the public did not know who Joe Biden was. Hillary Clinton, his main rival, was extremely popular at the time, with 100%

awareness from the public. Opinion polls were also not doing well compared to the other candidates. Most of the stats put him in 4th place among his fellow democrats: Edwards, Obama, and Clinton.

There was also the issue of experience versus change. Biden cited his 34 years of experience in the senate. He had actively participated in several congressional committees, including serving as the chairman of the Judiciary Committee and the United States Senate Committee on Foreign Relations. He also spoke about his role in resolving the conflict in Bosnia. This experience, he hoped, would help restore America as the leader of the world. What America needed, he suggested, was a leader who was capable of action – someone who would be able to take the necessary steps to end the war.

Chapter 7: Vice President

Shortly after stepping out of the presidential race, Barack Obama approached Biden privately with an offer for the vice presidency if he won the election. Would he be interested in running beside him? Biden initially rejected the offer because he saw it as a step down from the Senate seat, but he accepted after some thought.

Some sources, such as the New York Times, suggested that the idea behind the selection was to have someone with experience in national security and foreign policy on the team. Others claimed it was to emphasize the "change" message in the Obama campaign. Some said it was to appeal to blue-collar and middle-class voters, while others added it was because he was willing to challenge John McCain aggressively, who was the main Republican nominee. Whatever the reason, Biden received the official nomination in Denver on 27 August at the Democratic National Convention.

Soon after, some Catholics heavily criticized him for supporting abortion rights. His church, the Roman Catholic Diocese of Wilmington, actually barred him from speaking at catholic schools. Even his hometown bishop at Scranton, Pennsylvania, prohibited him from taking Holy Communion.

Liberal catholic and democratic campaign groups began scrambling for swing state catholic votes in Scranton. Liberal Catholics pointed out that there were much more important things to worry about. Many conservative Catholics and bishops believed that abortion was paramount. Biden explained that he believed life began at conception, but he did not want to force his religious beliefs on anyone.

Meanwhile, on the political stage, it was Joe Biden vs. Sarah Palin, the Alaska Governor running with the Republican vice presidential ticket. At first, Palin's popularity surpassed Biden's by miles. This was because the media was paying most of their attention to the Republican running mate, with research showing that Biden received only about 5% of the total media coverage during the race. So he took his campaign to the poorer parts of swing states and tried to appeal to blue-collar Democrats, particularly those who had previously been Hillary Clinton supporters.

During the final days of the campaign, Biden focused on older, less-populated, economically challenged areas such as Pennsylvania, Ohio, and Florida where he was popular, but Obama had not explored. In the end, the strategy appeared to have worked, because on 4 November 2008, the Obama/Biden ticket won the popular vote by 54% and the electoral vote by 365-173. Biden was officially the 47th U.S. Vice President.

According to Delaware law, you can run for Senate and vice president simultaneously, and so Biden did – for the seventh time. On 4 November, he beat Republican Christine O'Donnell to clinch the Senate seat as well.

At the beginning of Obama's first term, Biden served as a behind-the-scenes counsellor. He was highly influential in getting support from the senate when it came to passing certain important legislation pieces and actually helped convince Republican senator Arlen Specter to jump over to the Democratic side. Given his track record on foreign policy, President Obama also decided to leave Biden in charge of handling Iraq's situation.

One of Biden's biggest accomplishments as vice president was overseeing the 2009 economic recovery. It was the biggest task he had ever had so far, and it involved a government-spending program with up to $800 billion intended to lift the country from a devastating depression. There were 28 federal agencies with 275 programs and at least 100,000 projects. It involved scores of bureaucracies and minding several minor details. Naturally, some public officials were bored. But Biden took on the task with a zeal that those who were by his side recall with pride. Jared Bernstein, Biden's old economic adviser, said that Biden would be the most tested president when it came to the economy – even more so than FDR during the Great Depression because he was the main implementer.

In an interview with CNN, Biden recounted how he had to manage the project every single day. He would spend 3-4 hours a day on the phone, consulting with his team about the project's implementation. Some critics said that he should have made the stimulus package bigger. However, keeping it under the $1 trillion mark was the only way to get the Republicans to pass the Senate bill. Others (the Republicans) said that he was focusing too much on

Democratic priorities instead of trying to gain GOP support. However, the democrats retorted that the House GOP had opposed the plan before it even reached Capitol Hill in the first place. It was mainly thanks to Biden's ability to convince 3 Republican Senators – Pennsylvania's Arlen Specter and Maine's Susan Collins and Olympia Snowe – that the Obama administration could pass any program at all.

When Obama took office, the unemployment rate reached 8%, with 800,000 people losing their jobs. This was worse than when defence factories stopped operating after World War 2. In the stimulus, Obama proposed a mixture of infrastructure programs, food stamp expansion, aid to local and state governments, tax credits for business, and tax cuts.

The president called for the efficient running of the program. In February 2009, Biden gave him a memo over lunch detailing his proposal to manage the project. After a glance, Obama returned the memo and remarked, "Great, do it."

Biden was highly involved in the program because he knew there was so much on the line, including his very reputation. Previously, people knew him for promoting and hiring competent staffers, a strategy that he hoped to use in this task. During the first two years, he called twenty-two cabinet meetings to discuss the economic recovery program. This was not typical of a V.P., and actually surpassed the president's meetings on all topics. Biden also met with mayors and governors 57 times and barred 260 suspicious projects from sketchy contractors and other shady sources.

He was hands-on from the word go, always checking up with his staff to ensure the provision of necessary updates to local and state officials. He put Earl Devaney in charge of weeding out suspected waste. Devaney was the former inspector general of the Interior Department and the former head of the fraud division at the Secret Service. Ed DeSeve, who had a lengthy background at the office of Management & Budget during the Clinton presidency, took over the program's day-to-day running. In the end, Biden was able to shepherd the effort to completion without any incidence of fraud, even if it did not receive much political credit or praise at the time.

In October 2010, Joe Biden announced that he would be running with President Barack Obama for the second term. Earlier, there were rumours that Hillary Clinton would replace Biden for the Vice Presidential ticket, but Obama has never confirmed those claims. Nevertheless, Biden was still a valuable member of the Obama campaign who could appeal to disaffected, rural residents, and blue-collar workers. Therefore, as the campaign took off, Biden made several trips to the swing states to try and gain some more votes.

During the vice-presidential debate against Paul Ryan of the Republican Party, Biden made an inspiring defence of Obama's administration in a bid to regain some points after Obama's unconvincing debate against Mitt Romney. On 6 November 2012, Biden and Obama sailed through to their second term by winning both the popular vote (by 51%) and Electoral College vote (by 332 to 206).

Chapter 8: Presidential Hopeful

Biden's appeal in the Trump era is clear; he has the authority and experience President Trump lacks, having served as a vice president for eight years and senator for 36 years.

His approach to dealing with coronavirus, the global pandemic currently affecting the country, is to hire 100,000 staff to establish a national program for contract tracing and provide free COVID-19 testing for everyone. He aims to set up ten or more testing centres per state and has recently encouraged governors to mandate wearing masks.

One of the major impacts of the coronavirus pandemic is the loss of jobs and money. To address this, Biden has proposed to add more direct payments to families and to boost small businesses with loans. He has also suggested increasing monthly social security payments by $200, forgiving federal loans to students by up to $10,000, and rescinding tax cuts authorized by the Trump administration.

On a broader economic scale, Biden hopes to appease blue-collar workers and young people, two groups that have always had his back throughout his political career. As such, he has voiced his support for increasing the minimum wage to $15/hour – a measure that the young people are eagerly anticipating. Additionally, he wants $2 trillion to be invested in green energy to create more jobs for the working class. He has also been a strong advocate of "Buy American" laws, and his plan calls for a $300 billion investment in US-made technology, research, materials, and services.

On the issue of racism, Biden said he believes that one way of dealing with racism is establishing broad social and economic programs to support minorities. As a result, he hopes to use $30 billion to provide minority groups with business support.

His outlook on criminal justice has changed since the 1990s, where he received criticism for his "tough-on-crime" stand. He would now introduce policies to rehabilitate ex-convicts, address income and gender-based discrepancies in the justice system, and reduce incarceration. He proposes creating a grant program with $20 billion to encourage states to eliminate the death sentence, expunge previous cannabis convictions and decriminalize marijuana, and reduce the rate of incarceration. However, he does not believe in defunding the police and insists that there is a need for resources to maintain standards. For example, he suggests investing some of the funding in social services such as mental health.

When it comes to global climate, Mr. Biden says that Trump's exiting from the Paris Climate Accord was a mistake. He plans to re-join the agreement, in which the U.S. committed to cut greenhouse emissions by up to 28%. He proposes investing $1.7 trillion on green technologies research spread over the next decade and hopes that the U.S. will reach net-zero emissions in the next thirty years. Sixty more countries have made the same commitment. India and China are noticeably absent from the deal, considering they are two of the biggest carbon emitters.

Over the course of his career, people have known Joe Biden mainly for his foreign policies. As president, he aims to prioritize national interests first. However, he has vowed to maintain his strategy of engagement and multilateralism on the world stage. He hopes to repair severed relationships with U.S. allies, especially the NATO alliance. According to the former vice president, China should take responsibility for their unfair trade and environment practices.

When it comes to healthcare, he aims to expand Obama care, which was implemented during his vice presidency under President Barack Obama, to insure up to 97% of Americans. Although he disagrees with universal health insurance provisions, all Americans will have the option to apply for a public health insurance service such as Medicare, which covers the elderly. Biden also aims to make the age of eligibility 60 instead of 65, which would total the plan to about $2.25 trillion over one decade.

Biden has indicated that he would reverse some of Trump's policies separating children from their parents at the Mexican border and rescind travel bans on several Muslim-based countries.

In terms of education, Biden has endorsed many significant education policies that are popular among the democrats. These include universal preschool access, expansion of tuition-free colleges, and student loan debt forgiveness, which the money obtained from withdrawing the tax cuts authorized by Trump will cover.

Biden's record of deal-making, including negotiating budget deals and Ukrainian ceasefires, and helping pass a ban on assault weapons as vice president, shows a unique type of determination needed in the White House. His inspiring back-story and uplifting rhetoric prove he may be able to draw back the middle-class voters who sided with President Trump at the 2016 election. His supporters claim that he has enough clout to lure back Trump voters and sufficient credentials from his vice presidency days to appeal to the Democratic base.

But critics have presented several weaknesses to his presidential candidacy. These include the gaffes, like telling a crowd of African Americans that Mitt Romney wanted to put them "back in chains," or asking a crippled politician to get up for applause. These actually have their own term – Bidenism, also known as the art of publicly humiliating yourself and other prominent individuals.

There is also the issue of accountability. How can Joe Biden prove that he is not a part of the swamp when he has spent almost 50 years in public office? Most recently, several women also brought sexual assault allegations against Mr. Biden, including one Tara Reade. Reade alleged that the former vice president had sexually assaulted her in an office building at Capitol Hill back in 1993. Specifically, Reade alleged that Biden had stopped her in a corridor after delivering a package, pressed her against the wall, and digitally penetrated her.

Reade, who identifies as a domestic violence lawyer and advocate, stated that the violent physical and emotional abuse she endured from her ex-husband and father inspired her passion for her work. Reade was Joe's Congressional aide from 1992 to 1993. Her testimony has drawn criticism after misrepresenting herself multiple times, including lying in court proceedings while under oath. For instance, she lied that she had a bachelor's degree from Antioch University, at which she occasionally taught as a visiting professor. Her validity was further tainted after it was discovered that she had lied about her qualifications when applying for law school, allowing her to pursue a law degree without passing the required standards. Because of lying about her educational qualifications, Monterey County prosecutors are currently investigating her. Some Biden supporters claimed it was character assassination, as Reade had previously commented something that seemed to support the former vice president. For instance, she had made several tweets praising Mr. Biden just a few years prior. She had also re-tweeted and endorsed some of his posts, painting him in a favourable light.

A few other women also came forward with their personal stories, citing inappropriate contact such as kisses on the cheek, shoulder rubs, and hugs. Biden, responding to the allegations, said that he would be more careful next time about minding other people's personal space. The women later specified that his manner of touching was more a matter of unprofessionalism, tone-deafness, and poor judgment, rather than sexual harassment or assault.

Kamala Harris is Mr. Biden's running mate. She is the first black woman ever to appear on the presidential ticket of a major party. Ms. Harris has a lot of experience in Washington, is popular with the Democrats, and has a moderate view on important matters. She was also California's attorney general as well as its senator. She is known for her work as a prosecutor, as well as her centrist policies. Since she is a woman of colour, she gives credit to Mr. Biden's promise to enforce legislation to deal with racial inequality protests.

Kamala Harris was born in Oakland, California. Both of her parents are immigrants – her father is Jamaican while her mother was born in India. She grew up with her Hindu mother –a civil rights activist and cancer researcher – when the family broke up. As a result, she is well connected to her Indian roots – as she used to visit India regularly with her mother and her black culture from her Oakland upbringing.

Ms. Harris says that she identifies as an "American" and has always been comfortable with her identity. She added that you don't have to fit into a particular compartment based on your background or colour because you are a politician. She studied at Howard and has a law degree from the University of California. In her almost two terms as attorney general, the Democratic Party described Kamala Harris as a rising star. She went on to be elected junior U.S. senator for California in 2017.

Biden's campaign received a shot in the arm when he announced Ms. Harris as his running mate, thanks to donations from some of her wealthy friends and supporters in California. One of the factors that will determine Biden's odds of winning the presidency is his ability to win over young and progressive voters, who are more left leaning. This is coupled with the fact that Ms. Harris is a former prosecutor, whom most young people regard as a "cop."

There is another issue of age. If elected, Mr. Biden would be seventy-eight years old at the inauguration, just four years older than President Trump, which would make him the oldest first-term president in the history of the U.S.

However, Biden's surprising victory over Sanders in the primaries means that he is still a force to be reckoned with. His strength was not in his performance in the debates or campaign trail. He was not new and exciting like Pete Buttigieg or Kamala Harris, and neither did he have a half-billion-dollar budget like Michael Bloomberg to use on his campaign. Instead, he was a white, graying politician with over three decades of experience in the Senate and eight years as vice president, who could not raise enough money for his campaign. He clenched the victory mainly because of his ability to appeal to both old white voters and black voters.

As he is not running against Hillary Clinton this time, Trump will likely have a challenging time holding onto the white working-class voters, whose issues he has failed to address since his election in 2016. The current climate of economic dislocation amidst a global pandemic makes it difficult to ascertain his re-election chances, unlike most other incumbent presidents, considering that only three other presidents (George H W Bush, Jimmy Carter, and Herbert Hoover) failed to retain their seats in the last century. Like Bush, Carter, and Hoover, the weak economy may jeopardize Trump's re-election.

On the other hand, Biden has the advantage of steadiness and familiarity that voters are accustomed to.

But, only time will tell how everything will play out.

Joe Biden Timeline

1942 - Joe Biden Born

1961 - Graduated High School

1966 - Graduated Law School Married Wife Nelia Hunter

1972 - Won a seat in US senate fifth youngest senator ever elected

1972 - Wife and Daughter Die in Car accident

1988 - Failed Presidential Campaign

2002 - Votes for War in Iraq

2008 - Vice President Biden

2015 - Beau Biden dies age 46 from Brain Cancer

2020 - Third Run For President

Hope you enjoyed it. Click here to leave your review on amazon. Feedback of all kinds is appreciated.

[Click Here to leave my review](#)

WORLD CHANGING HISTORY

MANSA MUSA AND TIMBUKTU

A FASCINATING HISTORY FROM BEGINNING TO END

References

Promises to Keep: On Life and Politics

Barack and Joe: The Making of an Extraordinary Partnership
Joe Biden Unauthorized: And the 2020 Crackup of the Democratic Party

e

Made in the USA
Monee, IL
19 November 2020